TO: _____

FROM: _____

DATE: _____

Foreword

Black holes in space are a bit of a mystery: They have a mass so great, and a gravitational pull so strong, that even light cannot escape them. When an object hurtles past a black hole's "event horizon" (an invisible boundary that marks a gravitational point of no return), that object will be irretrievably captured. There is no going back.

In Romans the Apostle Paul tells us that everything in the created world is a metaphor for God's "invisible qualities, his eternal power and divine nature" (Romans 1:20). So, what if the dynamics of a black hole are a metaphor for our relationship with Jesus? What if our intentional movement toward him propels us past his "event horizon," making the gravitational pull of his orbit feel like a tractor beam? And what if this close orbit of Jesus finally restores the intimacy with God we were created to enjoy?

When Jesus drove away all the crowds that had been following him by insisting that they "eat his body and drink his blood," he asked his closest friends if they were going to abandon him as well. Because Peter had already crossed his own event horizon with Jesus, he answered this way: "Lord, to whom would we go? You have words that give eternal life" (John 6:68).

This is the response of a black-hole disciple of Jesus—one who is "ruined by him, and ruined for him." That person's life, forever going forward, will be characterized by intimacy with Jesus. And that life is possible for you as well, if you will allow this journal to propel you past his event horizon.

Rick Lawrence
General Editor, *Jesus-Centered Bible*
Author, *The Jesus-Centered Life*

How to Use This Journal

Drawn closely into Jesus' orbit—that's where life is both happiest and most exciting.

Expect to meet Jesus in fresh ways as you ponder passages pointing to him from both the Old and New Testaments. Ask what these verses can help you discover about Jesus... yourself...and your growing friendship with Jesus.

Just as in the *Jesus-Centered Bible*, blue passages are those from the Old Testament that point to Jesus, and red passages are those from the New Testament.

So journal well. Think deeply...doodle playfully... let your imagination send you soaring.

It's all good—because the Jesus who holds words of life and truth is eager to meet you anywhere, anytime.

John 1:1-3—"In the beginning the Word already existed. The Word was with God, and the Word was God. He existed in the beginning with God. God created everything through him, and nothing was created except through him."

Matthew 1:21—And she will have a son, and you are to name him Jesus, for he will save his people from their sins.

Deuteronomy 18:15-16a—Moses continued, "The Lord your God will raise up for you a prophet like me from among your fellow Israelites. You must listen to him. For this is what you yourselves requested of the Lord your God when you were assembled at Mount Sinai."

_____

_____

_____

_____

_____

_____

_____

_____

_____

_____

_____

_____

_____

_____

_____

_____

_____

_____

_____

_____

_____

_____

_____

_____

J. **Isaiah 61:1b**—The Lord has anointed me to bring good news to the poor. He has sent me to comfort the brokenhearted and to proclaim that captives will be released and prisoners will be freed.

_____

_____

_____

_____

_____

_____

_____

_____

_____

_____

_____

_____

_____

_____

_____

_____

_____

_____

_____

_____

_____

_____

_____

_____

_____

J. **John 6:35—Jesus replied,** "I am the bread of life. Whoever comes to me will never be hungry again. Whoever believes in me will never be thirsty."

_____

_____

_____

_____

_____

_____

_____

_____

_____

_____

_____

_____

_____

_____

_____

_____

_____

_____

_____

_____

_____

_____

Isaiah 11:2—And the Spirit of the Lord will rest on him—the Spirit of wisdom and understanding, the Spirit of counsel and might, the Spirit of knowledge and the fear of the Lord.

_____

_____

_____

_____

_____

_____

_____

_____

_____

_____

_____

_____

_____

_____

_____

_____

_____

_____

_____

_____

_____

_____

_____

_____

_____

J. **Matthew 11:28**—**Then Jesus said,** "Come to me, all of you who are weary and carry heaven burdens, and I will give you rest."

J. John 1:18—No one has ever seen God. But the unique One, who is himself God, is near to the Father's heart. He has revealed God to us.

_____

_____

_____

_____

_____

_____

_____

_____

_____

_____

_____

_____

_____

_____

_____

_____

_____

_____

_____

_____

_____

_____

_____

J. **Isaiah 40:11**—He will feed his flock like a shepherd. He will carry the lambs in his arms, holding them close to his heart. He will gently lead the mother sheep with their young.

_____

_____

_____

_____

_____

_____

_____

_____

_____

_____

_____

_____

_____

_____

_____

_____

_____

_____

_____

_____

_____

_____

J. **Matthew 8:26**—Jesus responded, "Why are you afraid? You have so little faith!"
Then he got up and rebuked the wind and waves, and suddenly there was a great calm.

_____

_____

_____

_____

_____

_____

_____

_____

_____

_____

_____

_____

_____

_____

_____

_____

_____

_____

_____

_____

_____

_____

J. **Isaiah 53:2b-3a**—There was nothing beautiful or majestic about his appearance, nothing to attract us to him. He was despised and rejected—a man of sorrows, acquainted with the deepest grief.

_____

_____

_____

_____

_____

_____

_____

_____

_____

_____

_____

_____

_____

_____

_____

_____

_____

_____

_____

_____

_____

_____

_____

_____

J. **John 17:3**—"And this is the way to have eternal life—to know you, the only true God, and Jesus Christ, the one you sent to earth."

_____

_____

_____

_____

_____

_____

_____

_____

_____

_____

_____

_____

_____

_____

_____

_____

_____

_____

_____

_____

_____

_____

J. Isaiah 11:10b—The heir to David's throne will be a banner of salvation to all the world. The nations will rally to him, and the land where he lives will be a glorious place.

John 5:24—"I tell you the truth, those who listen to my message and believe in God who sent me have eternal life. They will never be condemned for their sins, but they have already passed from death into life."

_____

_____

_____

_____

_____

_____

_____

_____

_____

_____

_____

_____

_____

_____

_____

_____

_____

_____

_____

_____

_____

_____

J. Matthew 16:15-16—Then he asked them, "But who do you say I am?" Simon Peter answered, "You are the Messiah, the Son of the living God."

J. Philippians 1:21—For to me, living means living for Christ, and dying is even better.

J. Isaiah 28:16b—"I am placing a foundation stone in Jerusalem, a firm and tested stone. It is a precious cornerstone that is safe to build on. Whoever believes need never be shaken."

_____

_____

_____

_____

_____

_____

_____

_____

_____

_____

_____

_____

_____

_____

_____

_____

_____

_____

_____

_____

_____

_____

J. 1 Timothy 2:5—There is one God and one Mediator who can reconcile God and humanity—the man Christ Jesus.

J. Romans 10:9—If you openly declare that Jesus is Lord and believe in your heart that God raised him from the dead, you will be saved.

_____

_____

_____

_____

_____

_____

_____

_____

_____

_____

_____

_____

_____

_____

_____

_____

_____

_____

_____

_____

_____

_____

_____

J. 1 John 5:5—And who can win this battle against the world? Only those who believe that Jesus is the Son of God.

J. Revelation 1:5—Jesus Christ…is the faithful witness to these things, the first to rise from the dead, and the ruler of all the kings of the world.

_____

_____

_____

_____

_____

_____

_____

_____

_____

_____

_____

_____

_____

_____

_____

_____

_____

_____

_____

_____

_____

_____

J. 2 Corinthians 12:7b-9a—I was given a thorn in my flesh…Three different times
I begged the Lord to take it away. Each time he said, "My grace is all you need.
My power works best in weakness."

Romans 5:6—When we were utterly helpless, Christ came at just the right time and died for us sinners.

J. Philippians 2:6-8—Though [Jesus] was God, he did not think of equality with God as something to cling to. Instead, he gave up his divine privileges; he took the humble position of a slave and was born as a human being.

_____

_____

_____

_____

_____

_____

_____

_____

_____

_____

_____

_____

_____

_____

_____

_____

_____

_____

_____

J. John 10:27-28—"My sheep listen to my voice; I know them, and they follow me. I give them eternal life, and they will never perish. No one can snatch them away from me."

John 14:6—Jesus told him, "I am the way, the truth, and the life. No one can come to the Father except through me."

J. Acts 13:38b-39a—"We are here to proclaim that through this man Jesus there is forgiveness for your sins. Everyone who believes in him is made right in God's sight."

John 8:31-32—Jesus said to the people who believed in him, "You are truly my disciples if you remain faithful to my teachings. And you will know the truth, and the truth will set you free."

J. **John 6:40**—"For it is my Father's will that all who see his Son and believe in him should have eternal life. I will raise them up at the last day."

J. John 8:57-58—The people said, "You aren't even fifty years old. How can you say you have seen Abraham?" Jesus answered, "I tell you the truth, before Abraham was even born, I am!"

John 12:44-45—**Jesus shouted to the crowds,** "If you trust me, you are trusting not only me, but also God who sent me. For when you see me, you are seeing the one who sent me."

1 John 5:12—Whoever has the Son has life; whoever does not have God's Son does not have life.

J. **Deuteronomy 30:6**—"The Lord your God will change your heart and the hearts of all your descendants, so that you will love him with all your heart and soul and so you may live!"

1 John 4:15—All who declare that Jesus is the Son of God have God living in them, and they live in God.

J. **Luke 6:46**—"So why do you keep calling me 'Lord, Lord!' when you don't do what I say?"

_____

_____

_____

_____

_____

_____

_____

_____

_____

_____

_____

_____

_____

_____

_____

_____

_____

_____

_____

_____

_____

J. Matthew 17:5—But even as he spoke, a bright cloud overshadowed them, and a voice from the cloud said, "This is my dearly loved Son, who brings me great joy. Listen to him."

Luke 24:6-7—"He isn't here! He is risen from the dead! Remember what he told you back in Galilee, that the Son of Man must be betrayed into the hands of sinful men and be crucified, and that he would rise again on the third day."

Daniel 10:5-6a—I looked up and saw a man dressed in linen clothing, with a belt of pure gold around his waist. His body looked like a precious gem. His face flashed like lightning, and his eyes flamed like torches.

J. Matthew 27:37—A sign was fastened above Jesus' head, announcing the charge against him. It read: "This is Jesus, the King of the Jews."

Jesus-Centered Journal

New Living Translation

Copyright © 2015 Group Publishing, Inc.

Visit our websites: group.com and jesuscenteredlife.com

ISBN 978-1-4707-3919-5 Charcoal leather-like cover

ISBN 978-1-4707-3918-8 Turquoise leather-like cover

Printed in China.

10 9 8 7 6 5 4 3 2 1   24 23 22 21 20 19 18 17 16 15